The Science of Humanity

Five Fascinating Stories of People Who Helped Us Understand Ourselves

Nury Vittachi

Illustrations by Step Cheung

Contents

THE BOY WHO FOUND DIFFERENT WAYS OF THINKING

ABOUT 100 YEARS AGO, a boy called Jean Piaget sat and watched his mother. She was very clever, but he thought she often worried too much about unimportant things.

He never worried at all, and he was happiest when he was doing his hobby, which was collecting shells.

He loved his hobby so much that he contacted the local museum in his hometown of Neuchâtel in Switzerland for permission to visit after hours and look at the mollusks (that's the scientific name for creatures like clams, and squid and snails).

STEP C

But when he was about 10 or 11, he started thinking in a different way. He still didn't worry like his mother did, but he began to think in an analytical way, like an adult.

By the time Jean Piaget was 13, he was writing lots of scientific papers about mollusks and sending them to science journals. They printed them, not realizing that he was a child. They probably thought he was Professor of Snails at some university!

As you can imagine, this bright young man did well at school and university, and when he was in his 20s, he ended up helping a friend mark a large group of test papers.

While Jean was grading the answers, he noticed something. Children always made the same mistakes, and they were consistently different from the mistakes that teenagers and adults made.

And that was when he had the idea that would make him famous.

The mistakes that children made were not really wrong. They were right for the type of "logic circuits" in their brains. Their minds worked differently.

But at a certain age, their brains would start working like those of adults, and they would switch to giving the answers that adults gave.

Jean Piaget also thought about his mother. He realized that clever adults often worried too much, and he discovered the psychological term for it: she was neurotic.

These thoughts inspired him to become a psychologist.

He became a world expert on something called developmental psychology, specializing in the difference between children's brains and adults' brains.

He taught teachers that it was wrong to educate children as if they were little adults, making them sit in rows and take notes for hours.

Children learned through playing and having fun and using their imagination.

One of the reasons why classrooms around the world today include toys and games and storybooks and paintings and colorful posters is because of the findings of Jean Piaget.

Does your teacher sometimes tell you stories, or encourage you to draw pictures or do craft activities or play games? She may not know it, but she's putting into practice what Jean Piaget discovered.

STEP C

THE WOMAN WHO TAUGHT US LOVE AND REMEMBRANCE

ARTEMISIA WAS A PRINCESS. Cool job? Maybe not.

In the old days, princesses had few choices in their lives — and could not even choose who to marry. Love was not considered something to take seriously.

Princesses were given in marriage by their families to other rich families, to seal deals. Romance was never part of the deal.

But Artemisia the Second of Caria, a place which is now in a country called Turkey, was going to change that.

While still young, she married her own brother, a man named Mausolus. Now that might seem very weird to us today, but in those days, boys and girls were often raised separately, so it didn't seem odd to her.

In fact, she was madly in love with him, and he with her. They loved each other so much that people worried that if one of them died, the other would pine away, which means they would gradually die of sadness.

The truth would soon be known. Because Mausolus became sick and then he eventually did die.

Artemisia was so crazy with grief that people far and wide commented on the strength of her love. Writers wrote about it in history books.

She had her workers build a huge monument for the body of Mausolus, and called it a Mausoleum. His body was cremated, and every day she put some of his ashes into a drink and drank it.

But Artemisia was now ruler of the land, and had some responsibilities. Her kingdom was at war with a neighboring place called Latmus. Her generals had fought hard with the soldiers of Latmus but had achieved nothing.

"Let me see what I can do," said Artemisia.

She announced that she and the royal ladies were going to organize the most spectacular meeting to worship the gods (everyone welcome!) at a particularly beautiful location in the countryside. There would be music and dancers and a procession.

Large numbers of people came to join the spiritual gathering, including the men and women of Latmus. And as soon as they left their city gates, Artemisia's men quietly took over the place.

Many people said it was the sort of trick that would never have occurred to an army general, but was a smart move by a clever queen.

Artemisia was still sad, and each morning seemed to get weaker in spirit and body.

Her broken heart killed her in 350 BC, less than two years after the death of the man she loved. But even though she lived more than two millennia ago, we still remember her as the princess who taught the world some important lessons about humanity.

Marriages are not just about linking families. She showed how powerful love can be, and she showed that what some people might call "female thinking" could achieve what "male thinking" might fail at.

And to this day, people around the world use her word, mausoleum, to talk about any building designed to enable people to remember a great and much-loved person who has died. Artemisia taught the world how to love.

THE MOTHER WITH SIX BOYS AND SIX GIRLS

ERNESTINE AND FRANK WERE two English-speaking children who would come to the dinner table speaking French one day and German the next.

How come? That will be explained shortly.

Life was strange in their house. The pair would have a lot of people to practice their new languages with — because there were six boys and six girls in their family.

Yes! Twelve children in one family!

STEP C.

How did the parents manage? With difficulty, of course, since something as simple as a trip to a nearby playground would be extremely challenging to organize.

But the mum and dad of the Gilbreth family were amazing people. Mum (named Lillian) and Dad (named Frank) and their children lived in the USA and this true story took place about 100 years ago.

The amazing thing was that the Gilbreth parents were specialists in engineering and science, but soon found a specialty to make their own: efficiency.

They became famous as efficiency experts, and many of today's ideas in ergonomics (that's the science of achieving as much as possible with as little wasted effort as possible) came from their work. Lillian Gilbreth is now seen as the very first industrial psychologist.

Of course, people made a lot of jokes. It seemed as if the couple had had such a lot of children deliberately, to force themselves to be super-efficient every day of their lives!

Here are some examples. The mum, Lillian, worked out that people in kitchens moved in a triangular shape, from the sink to the cooker to the counter — and that information, when revealed in a book, became influential in kitchen design.

Another efficiency trick was to sometimes do two things at once. There would be language learning records playing in the bathroom while the children were using it — which explains why the youngsters would go to the bathroom to wash their hands, and then come to dinner speaking French and German.

When the family would go out, people would ask why they had so many children, and the Dad would joke: "It's cheaper by the dozen, you know." This was a standard line that sales people used in those days to encourage people to buy more items and get a discount.

When Ernestine and Frank, the two youngsters mentioned at the beginning of this report, grew up, they wrote a book about their hilarious family life. It was called "Cheaper by the Dozen".

The book has been made into a movie twice, the most recent one being a very funny film starring Steve Martin — do take a look if you get the chance.

But don't forget: that oversized family really existed — and was responsible for some of the most important work in the science of efficiency.

THE GIRL BORN IN THE SHADOW OF THE MOON GOD

ONCE UPON A TIME there was a beautiful princess who was the daughter of the High Priestess of the Moon God and a great warrior called King Sargon of Akkad.

That sounds like something out of a story book, right?

But in fact, that's a true story and exactly how history remembers a girl named Enheduanna (pronounced En-hed-u-ah-na).

She was born as the child of the High Priestess of the Moon God in a place which appears in history books as Mesopotamia.

STEP C.

Why? Because it may be one of the oldest female names in history. She was born in 2285 BC — more than four thousand years ago!

While there are lots of historical clues to what people were doing a long time ago, there are very few people whose names were written down, and the few who were, were nearly all men.

The name of her father, King Sargon, was written down, but archeologists are not sure about her mother's name. One explorer found a single piece of broken pot in the area with a name on it: Tashlultum. So that may have been the name of Enheduanna's mother. No one knows for sure.

Enheduanna was the name she took when she became a young adult and was appointed High Priestess of Innana, the goddess of love and war and wisdom and lust (what a combination!). Nobody knows what she was called when she was a small child.

But what she did that was important was to become a writer. She wrote poems and hymns and thoughtful essays about spiritual things. Her work survived and influenced many books through the ages. She may even be the earliest known author to have signed her books.

As a High Priestess, she had to help govern one of the regions of the country, which wasn't easy. At one time, she and her brother were deposed and had to work hard to get back into power.

Enheduanna would have heard stories of a famous earlier ruler of the land, a man called Gilgamesh, who lived a couple of hundred years before her, and who was said to have had a friendship with a strange creature who was half-man, half-monster.

She may have started writing a book about him, or inspired other people to do so. Because one of the most famous books in the world has been traced back to about 2100 BC, which is not long after her death.

The stories of Gilgamesh were eventually compiled into humanity's earliest surviving work of literature, and may even be counted as the first novel ever.

If you like reading (or writing) stories, say thank you to one of humanity's first named authors, Enheduanna, daughter of the High Priestess of the Moon God.

STEP C.

THE EXPLORER GIRL WHO TRAVELLED FAR WITHOUT LEAVING HOME

A TEENAGE GIRL CALLED Alice sat on a chair, gripped by a book.

It was called "The Merv Oasis", and it was the thrilling true story of an explorer called Edmund O'Donovan who went to a land called Persia and met people of all sorts of cultures living dangerous lives on the edge of the desert.

It was a high-risk part of the world — shortly after writing the book, the author went on another expedition and lost his life.

The girl snapped the book shut and made up her mind.

She was going to be a medical missionary and go to distant exotic lands to help people in need.

Alice knew it would difficult, since in those days, pretty much all doctors and explorers were men.

The first part of her plan went fine. Alice Hamilton, who had been born in 1869 in New York, successfully studied medicine and became a doctor. But where to go?

That's when she made a discovery.

There was no need to travel to exotic lands. There were plenty of people who needed her help in the poor areas of her own country.

In the early 1900s, factory workers, including children, were made to work on a range of items, including things made of lead and even radioactive materials!

Alice Hamilton knew a lot about science and made a huge fuss.

Bosses were failing to keep their workers safe, she thundered.

Other people had been saying the same thing, but since Alice was a medical doctor, she could produce scientific proof that radiation killed people — so people started to listen.

Alice Hamilton became a world expert on occupational health, and her influence spread around the planet.

Once she ended up in a courtroom trying to prove that something called "happy dust" that was being given to children was actually illegal cocaine.

So she dropped some into her eyes and showed the judges how it made the pupils dilate, which means the black part at the center gets bigger.

Today, whether you work in a school or a factory or an office, there will be some sort of "health and safety inspectors" who will make sure you won't be harmed by things around you.

Their existence was inspired by the work of Alice Hamilton and other occupational health experts. She changed the way society thinks about workers: it is now part of a boss's responsibility to make sure they are not putting their staff in hazardous situations.

She was the first woman to become a teacher at Harvard University, and in 1944, researchers decided to put her name on a famous list called "Men in Science"!

Even though she was a woman, she didn't mind. She knew that even though she had stayed in her own country, she had actually made a huge and important journey into an exotic place: she had entered a Man's World and she knew other women would follow.

For more on the same lines, check out Book 8 in this series, Women of Discovery.

KEEP READING

READING ABOUT THE LIVES of scientists and other discoverers adds to our store of knowledge, but we hope also leads us towards something much greater, which is wisdom.

This book is part of a series, which we hope you'll enjoy reading, and will spur you on to do your own scientific research.

The creators of this book wish you success in your explorations.

THE YOUNG SCIENTISTS SERIES

Book 1: SECRETS IN THE ROCKS
Five Astounding Tales of People Solving Mysteries Beneath Our Feet

Book 2: FABULOUS PHYSICS
Five Amazing Stories of People Who Solved Nature's Puzzles

Book 3: MAGICAL MATHEMATICS
Five Astonishing Stories of People Who Did Miracles with Numbers

Book 4: BREAKERS OF BARRIERS
Five Stunning Stories of People Demolishing Walls to Make History

Book 5: SCIENTIFIC PIONEERS
Five Incredible Tales of People Who Helped Develop the Scientific Method

Book 6: THE AMAZING QUANTUM
Five Awesome Stories of People Who Made a Revolution in Physics

Book 7: THE SCIENCE OF HUMANITY
Five Fascinating Stories of People Who Helped Us Understand Ourselves

Book 8: WOMEN OF DISCOVERY
Five Super Stories of Fabulous Females Who Made Scientific History

Book 9: THE INVENTOR'S SPARK
Five Marvelous Stories of People Who Helped Shape the Modern World

Book 10: ADVANCES IN ALCHEMY
Five Startling Stories of Chemistry and Biology

Book 11: THE CALL OF THE STARS
Five Wonderful Stories of People Looking to the Heavens

Book 12: MYSTERIES OF NATURE'S LAWS
Five Striking Stories of People Investigating the Deepest Puzzles of Reality

Published by

WS Education, an imprint of
World Scientific Publishing Co. Pte. Ltd.
5 Toh Tuck Link, Singapore 596224
USA office: 27 Warren Street, Suite 401-402, Hackensack, NJ 07601
UK office: 57 Shelton Street, Covent Garden, London WC2H 9HE

National Library Board, Singapore Cataloguing in Publication Data
Name(s): Vittachi, Nury, 1958– | Cheung, Step, illustrator.
Title: The science of humanity : five fascinating stories of people who helped us understand ourselves / author, Nury Vittachi ; illustrator, Step Cheung.
Other title(s): Young scientists series ; 7.
Description: Singapore : World Scientific Publishing Co Pte Ltd, 2017.
Identifier(s): OCN 969705206 | ISBN 978-981-3221-56-7 (paperback)
Subject(s): LCSH: Scientists--Juvenile literature. | Science--Juvenile literature.
Classification: DDC 509.22--dc23

British Library Cataloguing-in-Publication Data
A catalogue record for this book is available from the British Library.

All royalties received will be channelled to the National Book Development Council of Singapore (NBDCS) as a gift from the author.

First published 2017
Reprinted 2018

Printed in Singapore